S0-AAC-905

SCRATCH AND SPARKLE

HALLOWEEN
Activity Book

Step inside the spook-tastic world of
Halloween in this amazing book...if you dare!

Use your favorite pens and pencils to complete
the activities. Then go to the back of the book
to create dazzling masks and glittering crafts.

With a haunted house model to create,
a mix-and-match pumpkin patch, and much more!

make
believe
ideas

HOW TO USE YOUR SCRATCH-OFF PAGES:

At the back of the book, there are Halloween crafts for you to press out, create, and wear. Look for the crafts on the activity pages to see what you can make.

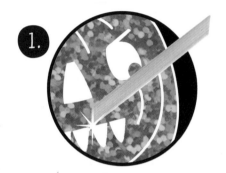

1.

2.

3.

Use the scratcher to give your crafts sparkling details.

Gently press out the shapes.

Finish the props with ribbon, glue, and some help from an adult!

CRAFT CONTENT

**Haunted house
See page 5**

**Pumpkin mask
See page 7**

**Monster mask
See page 9**

**Pumpkin patch
See page 11**

**Spider finger puppet
See page 23**

**Bat glasses
See page 25**

SPOOKY SPOTS

Circle the item that doesn't belong in each group.

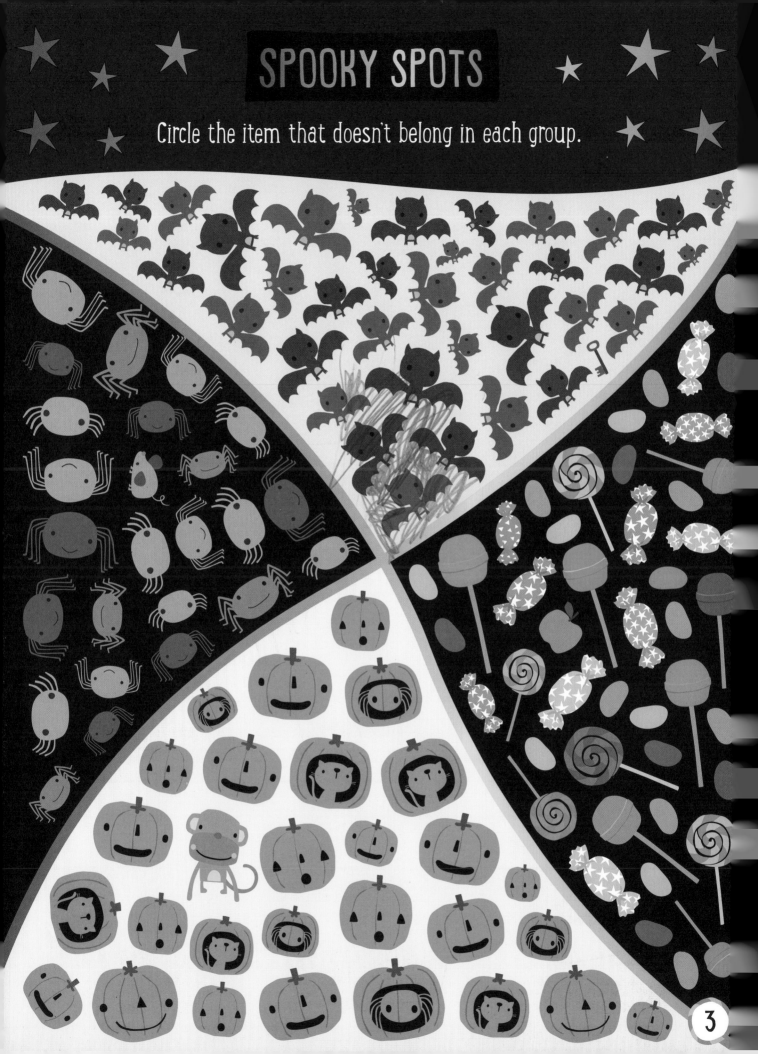

TRICK OR TREAT?

Guide the trick-or-treaters back home.
Collect all the candy along the way.

Start

Finish

SPOOKY MARKET

MAKE YOUR OWN HAUNTED HOUSE

1. Use the scratcher to add spook-tastic details to the house and characters.

3. Open the slots either side of the house. Fold the shape in half along the crease. Then push the house forward to make it 3-D!

2. Gently press out the house and character pieces.

4. Use your characters to bring the haunted house to life!

5

SUGAR SEARCH

Search the grid for the words below.
Words can go across or down.

 cake

 candy

 chocolate

 cookie

 lollipop

 popcorn

i	p	o	p	c	o	r	n	l	z
z	o	d	c	z	u	q	r	o	t
c	x	e	b	a	o	x	u	l	e
o	e	z	f	c	a	k	e	l	a
o	n	m	o	a	f	d	l	i	c
k	i	u	t	n	c	o	b	p	b
i	d	o	x	d	e	b	v	o	w
e	b	s	w	y	b	c	a	p	x
x	q	c	i	x	z	w	c	z	q
w	c	h	o	c	o	l	a	t	e

Decorate the trick-or-treat bag with color and doodles.

COLORFUL COSTUMES

Use color to finish the costumes.

MAKE YOUR OWN PUMPKIN MASK

1. Use the scratcher to add sparkly details to the pumpkin mask.

2. Gently press out the mask, eye holes, and small holes at either side.

3. Ask an adult to help you thread some ribbon through the holes and tie it around your head.

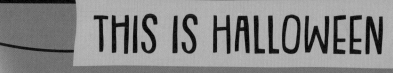

THIS IS HALLOWEEN

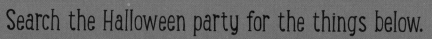

Search the Halloween party for the things below.

MAKE YOUR OWN MONSTER MASK

1. Use the scratcher to add fearsome details to the mask and mouthpiece.

2. Gently press out the shapes.

3. Ask an adult to thread some ribbon through the holes on the mouthpiece. Hold the mask in place and adjust the length of the ribbon, so the mouthpiece hangs in front of your mouth.

4. Now thread some ribbon through the small holes on the mask and tie it in place.

PICK-A-PUMPKIN

This pumpkin is being made into a jack-o-lantern.
Put the pictures in order by writing the letters.

A 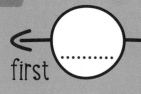   **B** 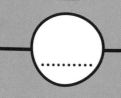   **C** 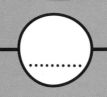   **D**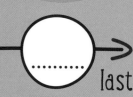

first 🔵 .... — 🔵 .... — 🔵 .... — 🔵 .... last

Use the key to solve the sums.

 =1   =2   =3   =4   =5

 + = ...

 + = ...

 + = ...

 +  = ...

 + = ...

 + = ...

10

Doodle scary faces on the pumpkins.

How many pumpkins can you count growing in the patch?

Write the answer. ....

MAKE YOUR OWN PUMPKIN PATCH

1. Use the scratcher to add sizzling details to the mix-and-match pumpkin patch and pumpkin faces.

2. Press out the pumpkin patch and open the slots. Then press out the pumpkin faces and open the mouth slots.

3. Slide the pumpkin faces onto the pumpkin patch. Mix-and-match to make some gruesome combos!

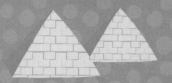

MUMMY MAZE

Color the treasure in the tomb. Then find the path to the exit.
You must go through every square once,
and avoid the spiders and webs!

SKELETON STREET

Decorate the skulls with color and doodles.

This skeleton is missing a bone. Can you find it?

13

ZOMBIE SWAMP

Read the description, and then circle five zombies hiding in the swamp.

WARNING!
ZOMBIES ON THE LOOSE!

Look out for:
-green skin
- open mouth
-ripped clothes

Finish the zombie.

HAUNTED HOUSE

Find and circle ten differences between the scenes.

Check the boxes when you find them.

1 2 3 4 5 6 7 8 9 10

PETRIFYING PETS

Follow the lines to discover which pet belongs to each trick-or-treater. Write the letters next to the owners.

CACKLE CORNER

Draw lines to match the joke to the punchline.
The first one has been done for you.

What do you call a werewolf with a fever?

What do witches put in their hair?

What is a ghost's favorite dessert?

What kind of music do mummies like most?

What kind of cough medicine does Dracula take?

Wrap music.

Scare spray.

Ice scream.

Coffin medicine!

A hot dog.

WEREWOLF WATCH

When do werewolves like to play?
Use the key to crack the code and write the answer.

A	B	C	D	E	F	G	H	I	J	K	L	M

N	O	P	Q	R	S	T	U	V	W	X	Y	Z

Find the one that doesn't belong.

20

Circle the silhouette that matches this picture.

1

2

3

4

Which square doesn't belong in this picture? Write the answer. ....

 A

 B

 C

 D

Answers: Werewolves play at the full moon; picture D doesn't belong

CREEPY CREATURES

What is there more of?

BATS:

(..........)

CATS:

(..........)

Use the grid to copy the owl. Then color it in.

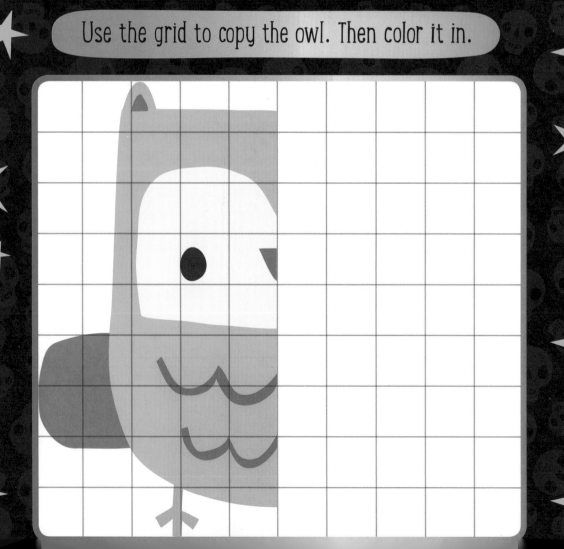

22

Color the sections with skulls in them purple to discover what creature is hiding here.

MAKE YOUR OWN SPIDER FINGER PUPPET

1. Use the scratcher to add glittering details to the spider shape.

2. Gently press out the spider shape and finger holes.

3. Put your fingers through the holes to bring the spider to life!

VAMPIRE CASTLE

Search the castle for the things below. How many can you see? Write the answers in the circles.

(5) bats  candied apples 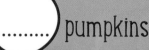 pumpkins ( ) cats

.... vampires   .... spiders

MAKE YOUR OWN BAT GLASSES

1. Use the scratcher to add daring designs to the bat frames and arms.

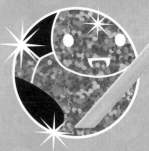

2. Gently press out the frames and eye holes. Fold along the crease and open the slots.

3. Now press out the arms and open the slots.

4. Slide the arms onto the frames to finish your bat glasses. Then put them on!

MONSTER MAYHEM

Draw lines to connect the close-ups
with the correct monster.

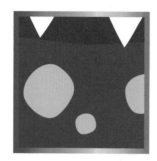

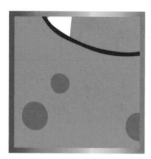

Finish the sums to see who has
scared the highest number of people.

A $1 + 2 =$ ....

C $3 + 2 =$ ....

B $2 + 4 =$ ....

D $2 + 2 =$ ....

Which monster has scared the most people? Write the answer. ....

26

Answer: B

Circle the pictures to answer the questions.

Who is sleeping?

Who is holding a lollipop?

Who is sad?

Who is singing?

Who is wearing a bow?

Who is upside down?

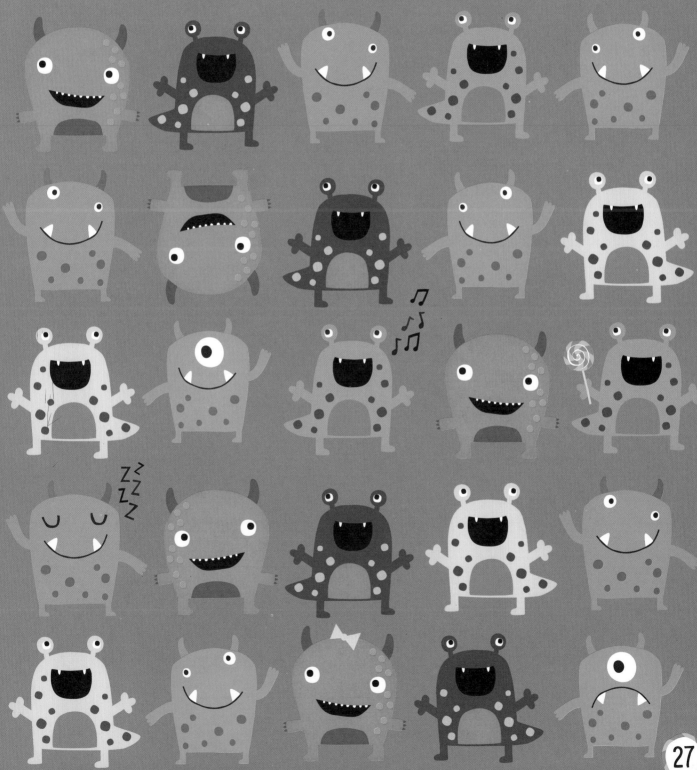

GHASTLY GHOULS

Join the dots to finish the ghost.

Trace the letters.

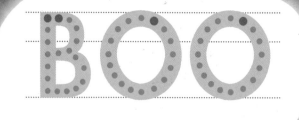